TWO LIVES

A FAITH-FILLED PATH TO HEALING AND HOPE IN SEASONS OF SORROW AND STRUGGLE

JOY BUTTS

Two Lives

ISBN Paperback: 979-8-9948168-0-6
ISBN Hardcover: 979-8-9948168-1-3

Dedication

This story is dedicated to every woman who's on a path of grief and purpose. Know that you are not alone as we embark on this journey together.

Acknowledgments

My sincere gratitude goes to:

God who has given me the strength to endure this journey.

My loving husband whom I am forever grateful for in my life.

My family and Kehilah[1] who have always been a source of great comfort, strength, growth and support.

My community for always lifting me up.
"We draw strength in community as we realize we are not alone on this journey"

—Joy B.

Holding you all near and dear to my heart.

I'm thankful for every lesson, every struggle and every blessing I've been invited to face on this glorious journey called life in Christ on this side of eternity.

---

1 Community

Table of Contents

Introduction

I'm sharing my story to expose and bring to light a hidden side of our humanity. There are times when what you see cleverly conceals the true reality lurking within. Externally, we appear polished, put together, well-groomed, and held together by many things.

Yet the question remains: Who are we, really?

What goes on behind closed doors in secret before the tears dry and make-up is applied? Who are we when we wake up late at night, terrified for tomorrow, scared of being exposed? Scared that the world will realize we're not as put together as we seem!

I'm here to tell you that this reality is a part of the human experience. We're in a time when profound grief, insecurity, shame, pain, panic, fear, and the list goes on and on, are hidden behind the mask of our smiles.

Take a moment and lean in as I share my story of pain and heartache to restoration and life. Transparency has always been taboo in our society, but I choose exposure and vulnerability. I invite the whole world to see what is hidden behind the smiles.

Are you willing to journey with me as we explore the reality of our weakness, while simultaneously discovering the strength we possess deep within?

A friend once told me, *"...some journeys we experience in secret with God, others we experience with a select few and others we experience with the collective."* For me, my journey has been experienced with the first two peering in. It is my honor and privilege to now share it with you in hopes of inspiring confidence as you embrace your journey.

And remember, you are not alone as we explore the ***"parallels of success amidst turmoil"*** together.

PART 1
Dear Reader

"Arrested to be honest, I am willing to be exposed for the possibility that you may gain liberty."

—Joy B. (Inspired by Galatians 5:13)

Chapter 1:

Tumultuous Beginnings

It was 2009 and I had just secured a new job with a major corporation. We had a month-long training out of town and my excitement to begin was palpable.

My husband and I had been married for 5 years and while I was excited about this new adventure, the desire for children began tugging hard on our hearts. We knew it was time to grow our family. However, career mobility was also knocking on the door. "Could we do both?" was the question that would soon be answered. Every weekend I'd come home after a week away for training. It was a grueling routine but we were both on board.

One early morning, about halfway through training, away from my husband, I awoke and something was terribly wrong. As I sat on the toilet, a strange thing happened. No matter what I tried, I couldn't relieve myself. At first I thought to stand up, brush my teeth and then try again in a few minutes. But the same thing occurred, only this time my stomach began to expand, getting larger and larger by the minute. Calming my panicked mind with a few prayers, I reached for the phone and dialed 911. Moments later, I was in an ambulance racing down the street, tears streaming down my face, ***alone!***

Amidst thoughts of panic, I pondered how embarrassing this was. Embarrassing because here I was away at a work engagement, trying to excel in my career with a major company. How would this look? Looking back, I'm shocked at how misplaced my priorities and thinking were. However, I was young, and the gift of hindsight can truly be a great teacher. This experience and many others have given me the courage to share with you today.

Wheeled into the emergency room and one catheter later, *"ahhhh sweet relief."* The doctor entered and said, "We need to operate."

"What!" I exclaimed with great concern. He went on to explain that several growths had infiltrated my uterus and grown to the size of a small unborn child. This benign growth, this fibroid that has plagued many a female, had pushed everything inside me around, crushing my urethra and rectum and resting close to my spinal cord. No wonder I could barely finish a full meal or feel comfortable siting down sometimes, or...the list goes on and on. At that moment, everything I had been going through finally made sense. Anger rose within and then quickly dissipated as my exhausted body and mind gave way to sleep.

Oh my goodness! What would I do? Will I be able to get pregnant? Have our dreams of childbearing been stolen? These were some of my thoughts when I awoke.

"This experience and many others have given me the courage to share with you today."

— Joy B.

A Poetic Interlude:

The Serpent

Slithering its way all across the canvas of your life, he takes hold, intricately weaving his slimy tentacles and tendrils into every portion of who you are to be.

Disappointed memory from so many years ago plagues you over and over and over again, like a broken record that just won't relent.

You sink into a level of comfort, living with the pain and the shame of the past, as he leans back, rejoicing with that silly, grimy smirk on his face.

You walk life out seemingly with victory, not realizing that the plan set so long ago has taken hold and the life you were meant to lead is no longer.

Duped!! You have been sieged and you didn't even realize it.

But then hope comes forth and the words of Isaiah spring up for new roads and streams to burst through the cage doors you have been stuck behind.

Behold I do a new thing; do you not perceive it? Roads in the wilderness I proclaim and streams in the desert places of your mind.

Renewed by fresh-water springs, an understanding of all things working together emerges.

Your bitterness dissipates like a vapor disintegrating on the breeze.

You are made fresh, you are made new, no longer held back by this massive wall of self-doubt and shame.

The serpent squeals its last breath as you clamp down, claiming victory like your Father proclaimed and facilitated through His Son so many years before when you were just a thought, a whisper in time.

"YOUR SEED SHALL BRUISE!!!"
—Genesis 3:15 ESV

"Victory is Mine!"

—Joy B.

Moment of Reflection

Experiencing setbacks in life can often feel like a profound pause, like the quiet before a great crescendo in a song. In times like these, if we take a moment to lean in, we can hear the faint whisper of a life lesson. This season of my life is ***when the pause became my teacher*** *and Jeremiah 29:11 helped anchor my heart within.*

Before proceeding, take a moment and reflect on how the scripture anchor and the reflection question below apply to your life:

____

____

____

____

____

____

____

____

____

Scripture Anchor

"For I know the plans I have for you, declares the Lord, plans for welfare and not for evil, to give you a future and a hope."
—Jeremiah 29:11 ESV

Reflection Question

Where is God inviting you to pause, not out of punishment, but for your protection and preparation?

Chapter 2:

Infertility 'the saga continues'

Relieved that the surgery was finally over, I thought, "Now the real healing can begin!"

Complications and scarring from the surgery left us with the question, "Can she get pregnant?" Yet, we were covered by faith in God's promises, which all at once flooded our minds: *You shall be fruitful and multiply, Genesis 1:28; your children shall be like olive plants round about thy table, Psalm 128:3; those who sow in tears shall reap in joy, Psalm 126:5.*

However, a new development was unearthed during our follow-up visit with the doctor. We had just discovered that it would be challenging for us to get pregnant because of all the scaring from the surgery. Our jaws dropped in shock at the news. It felt like the mighty blow of a gut punch that caught one off guard. We leaned on each other and drew strength as we took our petitions to God that night in prayer.

A few procedures later, I awoke to a season of extreme exhaustion. Unsure of what in the world was happening, I turned to the wise women in my life and shared how I was feeling. Like a boisterous chorus, they asked, ***Have you taken a pregnancy test?*** Cautiously optimistic, I scheduled an appointment with the doctor because we wanted to be sure there weren't any false results.

That weekend, surrounded by my expanded family at church, shouts of praise rang out in the midst of the congregation as we thanked God for answered prayer.

Persistent morning sickness followed for several months, becoming as much a part of my morning routine as brushing my teeth and getting dressed for work.

Let me back up a bit...

After the surgery and the healing period was over, I returned to complete my training for the new job. The training was a welcome distraction; however, the distraction didn't last long as I realized this particular work environment was just not the place for me. Less than a year later, I decided to leave that job for a new one with the hope that slowing my pace down and adjusting my life's rhythm would help with our dreams of becoming parents. A welcome sacrifice for a greater purpose. Beginning my career journey again, I was blessed to join another major corporation, where my new colleagues quickly became like a second family.

Now that you're all caught up, let's return to the dance of morning sickness.

Three months in and I was feeling a bit better as I settled into a new routine at the branch, serving clients as we awaited our glorious bundle of joy. Life couldn't be any better, besides the occasional blotting, loss of appetite and moodiness.

During this season I drew closer to God!

Push, Push, Push!

This can't be happening, it's too early!

Push, Push, Push!

I cried. This is really happening. Our baby was coming early, at around 24 weeks.

My husband was by my side, encouraging me as he looked in amazement at what the human female body can do.

Push, Push, Push!

And then I held him for the first time outside of my womb. A face so glorious, it looked just like my husband. Our shepherd (Pastor) comforted us as they took him away.

His life was brief and the joy of pain promised (John 16:21) was taken away as I was wheeled out from the midst of other families and other mothers and the cries of other babies—the joys of welcoming new life. I was left empty. No one prepares you for what awaits on the other side of this kind of pain.

"A woman giving birth to a child has ***pain*** *because*
her time has come; but when her baby is born, she forgets
the anguish because of her ***joy*** *that a child is born*
into the world."
—John 16:21 NIV

A Poetic Interlude:

Family

I grew up loving family! The intimate feel of everyday interactions, the grace of being born into a family brought to me by God. I love family!!

The warmth at the dinner table no one can feel anywhere else but home, where you make your bed and your heart can feast. Dining on the beauty of family!

The love that pours out each and every day in the hustle and bustle of life, like therapy, returning home, falling into the arms of the ones who love you, you're home again. Family!

Where, when it's just right, the pains of life's circumstances just cannot reach. Family! The first place you learn how to walk, you learn how to talk, you experience your first innocent kiss after the first date.

The place of bake sales and scraped knees, cupcakes and inside jokes that only family can make and believe. You are home!!!

A life of love and luxury wrapped up in mom, dad, sister, brother, aunty, friend.

What happens when it's ripped away and your heart is lost, tossed into the ether of confusion, not knowing where to go because the place that nurtured your soul is no more.

You hide inside, making a home in your soul, not letting anyone in for fear of rejection and pain!

Home has become a dark place, unable and unwilling to provide the same love and care you need because it's devoid of light.

That home in your heart nurtured by pain, oh so empty.

You have no place to go, so you run away, hoping that in this new place you'll find solace for your pain.

And then hope springs forth like the morning sun. The dawn awakes, and you blink your eyes, acclimating to the light of life within.

Home is no longer empty; it is filled with His love!! You know, the love of the One, the love of the Father, the love that knew you before landing on this earth.

TRUE LOVE, GOD'S LOVE!! Old, left behind, simultaneously birthed into new. Bringing forth something great you never could anticipate!

A love that never fails, a love that never gives up, ***LOVE***.

—Joy B.

Moment of Reflection

Have you ever experienced the disorienting effect of a thick white cloudy fog that rolled in all of a sudden, obscuring your vision and making what once was crystal clear, hazy? A disorienting experience, which the pain of this disappointment caused in my life. How in the world would I bounce back again was the question my fragile heart asked. And then, when despair almost finished making a home in my heart, unexplainable ***hope burst forth in the midst of the fog,*** *and I began to sing thanksgiving to my King. I knew this wasn't the end of the story.*

Before proceeding take a moment and reflect on how the scripture anchor and the reflection question below apply to your life:

____

____

____

____

____

____

____

Scripture Anchor

"Be anxious for nothing… with thanksgiving let your requests be made known to God."
—Philippians 4:6 NKJV

Reflection Question

What does it look like for you to hold hope even when outcomes are uncertain?

Chapter 3:

The Silent Years 'HOPE'

Thank God for our entire family who rushed to our side like blood to a wound, bringing life and resources in the form of prayers, encouragement, house cleaning, food prep, helping with domestic chores, and so much more.

There was a whirlwind of activity around my husband and I as I sat almost lifeless, retreating within, wondering what I would do. *Will I ever see the light of day again?* Days of numbness turned into weeks as the prayers of the righteous, which availeth (produces) much, buoyantly carried our family through (James 5:16).

Back at work, my colleagues, some of whom were pregnant at the same time, gently welcomed me back with love, caution, and compassion. My clients had no idea what had happened; therefore, understandably, *"congratulations!"* was the first thing they said with great joy and enthusiasm when they saw me. It almost broke my heart every time the words of what happened poured from my lips. It felt like opening a wound that had just begun to scar over and heal. An interesting experience, to say the least, of reliving the trauma all over again as I briefly shared what happened.

If it wasn't for the faith of God coursing through my veins, shrouding deep pain, which wasn't quite ready to surface, I don't know how I would have made it through. I'm forever grateful for the word of God hidden in my heart and guarding my life (Psalm 119:11 and Proverbs 4:23).

"Excuse me," I would say periodically during the day in order to retreat to a quiet space, the bathroom, and relieve my eyes from the flood of water they were holding back.

A splash to the face with cold water and I'd emerge once again, sometimes to rejoice with those who rejoice (Romans 12:5), celebrating their newborn. Don't get me wrong. I was genuinely happy for others, but I would be lying if I said it was easy. I needed a change and thankfully it came.

Settling into this new elevated posture of trusting God even in the face of tremendous adversity, I was blessed when the phone rang and a seed planted many moons ago sprang up. The voice of my soon-to-be manager mentioned an opening for a new position, and as you'd probably guess, ***I got the job!***

Excited for something new, I was even more elated that the daily reminder of the loss wouldn't be staring me in the face anymore. Full of hope I moved forward with God's redemptive plan for our lives in my gaze. The distraction of a rigorous onboarding process, a new mentor and constant travel was exactly what the doctor ordered for that season. And then, like a pervasive, persistent weed, the pain deep within would surface like clockwork year after year as my husband and I continued trying to bring forth new life.

Years later, we experienced the great joy of pregnancy again. We were so thankful. At this point, I was cautiously optimistic until rounding the corner of month five, when I gave my heart permission to enjoy the excitement of planning for this new adventure.

One early morning, lying in bed before work, I felt a rush of warmth all around me. My water broke, and the thought, *Not Again!* echoed in my mind like ricochet. Half asleep, my husband and I quietly looked at each other with heartfelt silence and compassion, as we got up to go to the hospital.

Whisked away to the hospital and wheeled down the corridor on a gurney like a piece of meat on a conveyor belt, I was half numb as the doctor said I was going to be admitted. I lay there in shock, husband by my side as he called my father, who was visiting, and then our pastor to tell them the news. Comfort and consolation calmed my soul as family drew near. And then we were left alone as night descended. I thank God for my amazing, attentive husband who was by my side the entire time. Like a mighty warrior at his post, he stood watch both physically and spiritually, keeping my soul at ease, my emotions at bay and my hope from wandering off never to return again. ***I am safe!***

Back in the delivery room, Push, Push, Push, words that were all too familiar and then ***SHE*** emerged. The room was silent as my head dropped back from sheer exhaustion, while morphine numbed the agonizing internal and external pain.

"Can I see her?" I asked, my words piercing the silence as I realized the defining void of silence, airwaves lacking the boisterous sound of tiny cries as she was laid to rest in the arms of the Father. And then the doctors said they hadn't gotten it all. Tubes were soon stuck down my throat so I could breathe while under the intoxicating influence of anesthesia, which quietly lulled me to sleep.

Could this all have been a dream? I thought to myself as I awoke. ***No!*** Unfortunately, not, I realize as I was wheeled back to my room, empty once again. That night was a night to remember. Cold shudders consistently woke me up as my loving husband spoke to my heart, calming me down, a gift the nursing staff marveled at as the Spirit of God within him and I calmed my soul.

Although the experience of delivering a child you would soon bury was familiar, mourning each loss was unique and came with its own challenges. This time, the crevice I dug, which God used to nurse my pain, was filled just a bit more with the soil of disappointment, and I wondered if I'd ever get out.

Meanwhile, on the other side of grief, the career ladder of "success" continued to steadily climb as the symphony of *"Tumultuous pain in the midst of great success"* became the theme music of my life. The search for meaning was particularly elusive, and the biblical proverb, "*It is the glory of God to conceal a matter and the glory of kings to search it out*" (Proverbs 25:2 ESV), became an altar my soul used to find rest.

Returning to life I began teaching the youth of our church, reminded every time of what we had lost while hopefully inspired for the future.

A Poetic Interlude:

Beautiful Smile

Beautiful smile, what's behind those **DARK EYES?**

Sparkling dazzling, what's veiled deep inside?

Perhaps a waterfall of tears, or a conflagration of shame, **NO!**

A boisterous flame burning inside, replacing deep pain.

It's **Hope** that you see raging within.

Resting quietly behind those beautiful dark eyes.

— Joy B.

Moment of Reflection

Grief coupled with hope and faith in God became my quiet companion and I emerged victorious!

Take a moment and allow the POWER of the scriptural promise below to settle deep within you and take root, then answer the reflection question:

____

____

____

____

____

____

____

____

____

____

Scripture Anchor

"The Lord is near to the brokenhearted and saves the crushed in spirit."
—Psalm 34:18 ESV

Reflection Question

How is God inviting you to honor both grief and gratitude in the same breath?

Chapter 4:

The Road to Success 'Unexpected Journey'

The corporate ladder I was climbing grew higher and higher as pain mixed with the healing ointment of God's presence got buried deeper and deeper within. Buoyantly floating on the sea of hope, my heart was steadied knowing that this wasn't the end of my story.

2020 approached, bringing with it a global pandemic, and a crushing blow of finality for our family. The ability to conceive, carry and birth new life was taken away, discarded in the trash of an RX bag, labeled *hazardous waste*. I was told by a myriad of experts that my womb would have to be removed or my health would suffer as a result.

The way in which many a female finds value and meaning, and several cultures and communities define a woman's purpose, was ***TAKEN!*** My supposed worth of femininity was relinquished as my supportive, grieving husband stood by my side. Fighting the good fight of faith is why my husband and I grew closer ***together*** rather than drifting apart.

And then the miraculous happened!

As I pressed into prayer and deepened my relationship with God, seeking holistic healing for my heart while serving in our youth ministry, He began to cultivate a renewed heart within me, one that would birth something new.

In this season of waiting, God gave me a promise of fruitfulness, one that would manifest in a way that I never expected. In the place of prayer, God gave me the words ***"Fruitful Barrenness."***

My most fruitful years began as I sought to understand the meaning of this God-given phrase: ***"Fruitful Barrenness."***

"Amidst a once lively womb ***Hope*** *is born*
as ***'fruitful barrenness'*** *is delivered."*
— Joy B.

Soon, I found my meaning, and the glory of kings was no longer concealed (Proverbs 25:2). I received the spiritual mandate to share my journey and pour into the next generation through the medium of story, expressed across multiple books, this one being the first.

Although I couldn't have a child of my own, I could birth possibilities through my words. The fruitfulness of writing came with such ease as I sat daily at my faithful, trusty desk, writing amidst a barren womb. This became a sacred way of escape for me, a place of comfort and peace, with more meaning than I could have ever imagined. Divine words penned through this earthen vessel (2 Corinthians 4:7-12) to nourish my soul, which would later facilitate healing for another's pain.

"Blessed be the God and Father of our Lord Jesus Christ, the Father of mercies and God of all comfort, who comforts us in all our affliction, so that we may be able to comfort those who are in any affliction, with the comfort with which we ourselves are comforted by God."
—2 Corinthians 1:3-4 ESV

"Fruitful Barrenness" emanated from deep within, and a new eternal ladder of success was born.

Virtually nurtured by a small group of close friends and family during the 2020 pandemic, my healing began as fossilized pain gave way to ***LOVE.***

I started to share my story with others to inspire and encourage them. Not too long after, my fragile heart was thrust into the limelight of interviews, national awards, and NBC specials in my new job. That's when God's words, He will never leave you or forsake you (Deuteronomy 31:8), became the ever-present promise my "God, I need You!" prayers stood on.

Five years later, I am blessed to share this joyous gift born out of pain with you (Proverbs 13:12). God always has a redemptive purpose and a plan, and sometimes, we can't see it.

But if we ***TRUST IN HIM!*** He will not and cannot fail. Sometimes the plan for God to prosper us with a future and a hope of an expected end (Jeremiah 29:11) looks different from what we anticipate. My prayer for you is that you remain open to **'*THE POSSIBLE!*'**

AS I END THIS LONG JOURNEY, I AM EXCITED TO BEGIN A NEW ONE full of adventure, new experiences and relationships along the way.

A Poetic Interlude:

Peace

In the distance amidst the storm, ***He*** was standing.
Such peace at the center as the winds blew all around me.
His hand stretched out waiting for me to say ***YES!***
I bravely took His hand and clung to His side.
Instant rest I would find, ***PEACE*** was now where I'd reside.
Yet my surroundings stayed the same.
Interactions and processes, those who knew me didn't change.
Yet I was different, and my task now is to be a guide leading others to ***His*** side.

A guiding light in the midst of the storm, leading others to Thy Light.
Light in a dark place, refuge in the midst.

Finding STRENGTH as you walk along with Him.

—Joy B.

Moment of Reflection

Fruitful Barrenness*—a question that led me on a tailspin of my greatest adventure yet. What does this word mean to you? What question may God be asking you? What adventure might He be inviting you to? Pause for a moment and ask Him. That's what I did and the answer opened the door I didn't even know was there.*

Before proceeding, quiet the noise and take a moment to reflect on the scripture anchor and the reflection question below. It may take you to places you've never dreamed.

Scripture Anchor

"It is the glory of God to conceal things, but the glory of kings is to search things out."
—Proverbs 25:2 ESV

Reflection Question

What story is God writing from the pages you wanted to rip out?

The best part of living…drinking in the Son!

Dear Reader,

Thank you for taking the time to lean in and read my story. It is my hope and prayer that you find yourself somewhere within its pages.

Perhaps you recognize yourself in the experience of a profound and unexpected loss, one that may have compounded over several years. Or perhaps you resonate with a shift in desire that altered the trajectory of your life, causing you to rethink what is truly important. Maybe you find yourself awakening to the realization that life is so much more than a career.

Wherever you find yourself, my prayer is that you are able to settle into the peace that only God can provide. A peace that doesn't disappoint, never fails and never fades. A peace that comes through total surrender to a life uniquely designed for you in Christ.

I invite you to continue this journey with me as we unpack what you have just read through a 40-day devotional created to offer a sacred space, one that supports rest, reflection and healing for your heart and soul.

May you enjoy the best part of living on this side of eternity by drinking in the Son (the Son of God, Jesus) and taking on His yoke, which is easy, and His burden, which is light, so that you may find true rest for your soul.

PART 2
The 40-Day Devotional

The Purpose in the Pause Devotional

Welcome to this 40-day devotional designed to take you through your own journey of reflection. This devotional is based on the application of the truth and power of God's word within my own healing journey. It is designed to meet you where you are. There are five major themes which you can go through chronologically, or thematically based on where you find yourself:

1. The Pause — When God Stops Us to Save Us
2. The Pain — When Loss Feels Like the End
3. The Process — Healing, Hope, and Holding On
4. The Purpose — Fruitfulness in the Unexpected
5. The Pursuit — Dream again

THEME 1:
The Pause – When God Stops Us to Save Us

Day 1 – The Sudden Stop
Jeremiah 29:11 – God uses divine pauses not to punish, but to protect and redirect.

Day 2 – Sacred Interruptions
Exodus 3:4 – What if the burning bush isn't a miracle, but a disruption asking for your attention?

Day 3 – When Dreams Delay
Proverbs 16:9 – Even detours have divine fingerprints.

Day 4 – The Pain That Speaks
Psalm 139:14 -Your body can reveal what your soul has been suppressing.

Day 5 – The Ambulance and the Altar
Romans 8:28 – Every ER visit, every lonely ride, every unanswered prayer—it's all seen.

Day 6 – Reordered Priorities
Matthew 6:33 – What matters most when everything else is stripped away?

Day 7 – Reframing the Pause
Isaiah 30:15 – In returning and rest… there's strength.

THEME 2:
The Pain – When Loss Feels Like the End

Day 8 – Grief Wears Many Faces
Ecclesiastes 3:4 – Tears are not weakness, they're sacred offerings.

Day 9 – The Silence of the Hospital Room
Psalm 22:1–2 – When God is quiet, He's not absent.

Day 10 – God in the Fog
Philippians 4:6–7 – Prayer doesn't always change things but it always changes us.

Day 11 – The Question No One Asks
Job 3:11 – Why? The question that echoes. The answer we may never receive.

Day 12 – Mourning in the Midst of Praise
Romans 12:15 – How do you clap for someone else's miracle while grieving your loss?

Day 13 – The Unseen Goodbye
John 11:35 – Jesus wept too.

Day 14 – Surviving Sacred Grief
Psalm 56:8 – God keeps every tear. None are wasted.

THEME 3:
The Process – Healing, Hope, and Holding On

Day 15 – The First Step Back
Isaiah 61:3 – God gives beauty for ashes but not always right away.

Day 16 – Courage in the Cubicle
Psalm 119:11 – Your workplace can become your prayer place.

Day 17 – The Ministry of Showing Up
Galatians 6:9 – Sometimes surviving is the victory.

Day 18 – Tears in Public Places
2 Corinthians 12:9 – Your weakness is where His strength shows off.

Day 19 – Healing is Not Hiding
1 Peter 5:10 – Every wound has a timeline. Let grace pace your recovery.

Day 20 – God of the Second Goodbye
Lamentations 3:22–23 – You survived the first. You will survive again.

Day 21 – Cautious Hope
Romans 15:13 – Hope that whispers, not shouts—but still hope.

THEME 4:
The Purpose – Fruitfulness in the Unexpected

Day 22 – Fruitful Barrenness
Proverbs 25:2 – What if your emptiness is fertile ground?

Day 23 – Birth Without Labor
Isaiah 66:9 – God still delivers. Just not always how we expect.

Day 24 – Writing Through the Pain
Habakkuk 2:2 – The pen can be the plow that turns your field of sorrow.

Day 25 – Your Story is Seed
John 12:24 – Unless a seed dies, it remains alone. But if it dies…

Day 26 – The Platform You Didn't Pray For
Ephesians 3:20 – God does more—sometimes through the wounds.

Day 27 – The Tribe You Didn't Know You Needed
Romans 12:4–5 – Healing often comes through community.

Day 28 – Redefining Success
Micah 6:8 – Maybe success is just obedience on repeat.

Day 29 – Glory in the Graveyard
John 11:25–26 – Resurrection doesn't just happen during Pesach (Passover)

Day 30 – Still Good, Still God
Romans 8:38–39 – Nothing—nothing—can separate you from His love.

THEME 5:
The Pursuit – Dream again

Day 31: Purpose in the Pause
Jeremiah 29:11 – Future plans

Day 32: Faith in the Fog of Grief
Philippians 4:6 – Prayer & thanksgiving

Day 33: When Hope and Heartache Collide
Psalm 34:17–18 – Close to the brokenhearted

Day 34: Fruitful Barrenness – When Pain Births Purpose
Proverbs 25:2 – The glory of kings

Day 35 – Redeemed & Rewritten
Romans 8:28 – All things work together

Day 36 – Hope Rushes In
Romans 15:13 – The power of the Holy Spirit

Day 37 – Hopeful Delight
Psalm 37:4 – The desires of your heart

Day 38 – Confident Hope
Philippians 1:6 – Completion…until the day of Christ Jesus

Day 39 – Rejoice
Romans 12:12 – Rejoice, be patient, be constant

Day 40 – Many Plans

Proverbs 19:21 – The Lord's purpose will stand

Days 36-40 provide you with the opportunity to write your own devotional as you find healing through the word of God, allowing the Holy Spirit to guide you in navigating the beauty of your own heart.

Opening Prayer

Before you start the devotional, please take a minute to say this prayer over yourself:

Lord, You have rewritten the meaning of suffering in my life. Where I saw dead ends, You whispered destiny. Where I only saw pain, You planted purpose. Thank You for sitting with me in silence, for speaking truth into my fog, and for never wasting a single tear. Help me to keep trusting, especially in the pauses. Especially in the barrenness. Because even here, You are good. Amen.

THEME 1:

The Pause – When God Stops Us to Save Us

Day 1: The Sudden Stop

Scripture:

"For I know the plans I have for you," declares the Lord, "plans to prosper you and not to harm you, plans to give you hope and a future."
— Jeremiah 29:11 (NIV)

Devotional Thought:

It happened suddenly. Life was moving forward—the schedule full, the goals set, the momentum steady. And then, everything stopped. An emergency. A diagnosis. A crisis that pulled you out of your flow and planted you in a place you never expected. It felt like punishment, like failure, like disruption. But what if it was protection? What if the sudden stop was God's mercy in disguise?

When God pauses our plans, He is often positioning us for something deeper, something richer. That ER room, that phone call, that loss—it may have looked like an interruption, but it was also an invitation. An invitation to trust. To realign. To listen.

Reflection Questions:

- Have you experienced a "sudden stop" that felt disruptive but was actually divine?
- What was God trying to show you in that moment?

Journal Prompt:

Write about a time when everything suddenly changed. How did it challenge your trust in God? What new understanding or purpose emerged in the pause?

Prayer:

God, when life stops suddenly and my plans unravel, help me not to panic. Remind me that You are still writing my story, even in the stillness. Teach me to lean into the pause, to listen for Your voice, and to trust that what feels like a setback may be setting me up for something greater. Amen.

Day 2: Sacred Interruptions

Scripture:

"When the Lord saw that he had gone over to look, God called to him from within the bush, 'Moses! Moses!' And Moses said, 'Here I am.'"
—Exodus 3:4 (NIV)

Devotional Thought:

What if the burning bush wasn't just a miracle but a divine disruption? Moses wasn't seeking a revelation that day. He was tending sheep, managing the ordinary. But God chose to speak through the interruption. Sometimes, we wait for signs and wonders, missing the quiet disruptions that are calling our name. The sacred often arrives disguised as inconvenience. Pay attention—God may be waiting in the detour.

Reflection Questions:

- How do I typically react to unexpected interruptions in my day?
- Could God be trying to get my attention through a current disruption?

Journal Prompt:

Write about a time when an interruption became a turning point in your life. What did you learn about God or yourself through it?

Prayer:

Lord, open my eyes to see You in the unexpected. When my routines are disrupted, help me pause and listen. May I not rush past the burning bushes You place along my path. Amen.

Day 3: When Dreams Delay

Scripture:

"In their hearts humans plan their course, but the Lord establishes their steps."
—Proverbs 16:9 (NIV)

Devotional Thought:

You thought you had it figured out—the timeline, the next step, the promotion, the breakthrough. But the delay arrived unannounced. Not as a gentle "not yet," but a crashing halt. Yet in the delay, God is not silent. He's re-scripting your next chapter with purpose.

Reflection Questions:

- How do I feel knowing that I will not always be in control of my life?
- What assumptions am I holding about God's timing?

Journal Prompt:

Describe a scenario when you felt out of control and how it made you feel. What did you do to cope?

Prayer:

Lord, help me to trust Your timing. When my plans are postponed, remind me that You are not procrastinating—You are preparing. Amen.

Day 4: The Pain That Speaks

Scripture:

"I praise You because I am fearfully and wonderfully made; Your works are wonderful, I know that full well."
—Psalm 139:14 (NIV)

Devotional Thought:

Your body is not just a vessel, it's a messenger. That tight chest, the fatigue that won't lift, the headache that keeps returning—these may be more than physical symptoms. Sometimes, pain speaks what the soul is trying to say. It is the Spirit of Truth, the Spirit of God, that longs to reveal the answer to your redeemed soul. All you need to do is answer His knock at the door of your heart, let Him in and allow His truth to penetrate and create in you a new spirit, and then the true healing can begin. You were created with intricate design, and your (spirit), emotions (mind and will) and body are deeply connected. Pay attention. God may be using your body to signal what your heart longs for and has tried to ignore.

Reflection Questions:

- What persistent physical symptoms might be pointing to emotional or spiritual pain?
- Have I been silencing my inner needs instead of addressing them?

Journal Prompt:

Reflect on a time when your body was trying to tell you something your heart wasn't ready to face. What did you learn through that experience?

Prayer:

Lord, thank You for fearfully and wonderfully creating me. Help me listen with compassion to what my body is saying. Heal not only my physical pain but the deeper wounds beneath it. Teach me to care for my whole self—body, mind, and soul. Amen.

Day 5: The Ambulance and the Altar

Scripture:

"And we know that in all things God works for the good of those who love Him, who have been called according to His purpose."
—Romans 8:28 (NIV)

Devotional Thought:

Every ER visit, every lonely ride in the back of an ambulance, every tear-stained prayer that seems to echo back with silence—it's all seen. These aren't detours; they're altars in disguise. Moments where heaven bends low, where God's hand is still steady even when ours shake. The chaos of the crisis does not cancel God's goodness. In fact, it's often the backdrop against which His purposes shine brightest.

Reflection Questions:

- Where in my life have I seen God bring good out of pain?
- How might I shift my perspective to see crisis as a potential altar?

Journal Prompt:

Recall a moment when everything felt like it was falling apart. Looking back, can you see how God was at work through it? What did you learn about Him—and yourself—in that moment?

Prayer:

God, in the moments that feel like emergencies, remind me that You are still in control. Help me see not just the flashing lights, but the flickers of Your purpose. Let every hardship become a place of worship, every ambulance a pathway to the altar. Amen.

Day 6: Reordered Priorities

Scripture:

"But seek first His kingdom and His righteousness, and all these things will be given to you as well."
—Matthew 6:33 (NIV)

Devotional Thought:

When the noise quiets and the plans fall through, what truly matters rises to the surface. Sickness, loss, or a moment of crisis has a way of stripping life down to its essence. Suddenly, what once felt urgent loses its grip, and what was overlooked—faith, family, peace—takes center stage. God uses these moments not to punish, but to gently reorder our hearts. To help us seek *first* what we often seek last: His kingdom.

Reflection Questions:

- What priorities have I placed above seeking God?
- In times of crisis or transition, what rises to the top of my heart?

Journal Prompt:

Think about a time when your life was interrupted or turned upside down. What did you find yourself clinging to most? How did that season shift your priorities?

Prayer:

Father, help me to seek You first—not just when life feels fragile, but every day. Reorder my heart so that what matters to You becomes what matters most to me. Strip away the distractions, and center me in Your truth. Amen.

Day 7: Reframing the Pause

Scripture:

"In returning and rest you shall be saved; in quietness and in trust shall be your strength."
—Isaiah 30:15 (ESV)

Devotional Thought:

We often view pauses as problems—interruptions to productivity or purpose. But what if the pause is the purpose? God's invitation to return and rest is not weakness; it's wisdom. In the stillness, He restores. In the quiet, He speaks. When movement stops, perspective sharpens. Sometimes strength isn't found in striving, but in surrender. And in the pause, God isn't withholding progress—He's offering presence.

Reflection Questions:

- How do I typically react to stillness or waiting?
- What might God be inviting me to notice or receive during a pause?

Journal Prompt:

Describe a season in your life when you were forced to slow down. What emotions did it stir in you? Looking back, what did God teach or reveal to you in that space?

Prayer:

Lord, help me to reframe the pauses in my life—not as setbacks, but as sacred invitations. Teach me to rest in You, to find strength not in rushing ahead, but in returning to Your presence. Quiet my heart and renew my trust. Amen.

THEME 2:

The Pain – When Loss Feels Like the End

Day 8: Grief Wears Many Faces

Scripture:

"A time to weep and a time to laugh, a time to mourn and a time to dance."
—Ecclesiastes 3:4 (NIV)

Devotional Thought:

Grief is not a one-size-fits-all emotion. It shows up as tears, silence, irritability, numbness, or even laughter that masks the ache. It's not confined to funerals—it comes in lost dreams, fractured relationships, unmet expectations. And every form of grief is seen by God. Tears are not a sign of spiritual failure; they're sacred offerings. He bottles each one, not rushing us past sorrow, but walking with us through it. There is healing in being honest about what hurts.

Reflection Questions:

- How do I tend to express or suppress grief?
- What would it look like to allow myself to grieve in God's presence?

Journal Prompt:

Write about a loss you've experienced—big or small—that you've struggled to name or grieve. What emotions have surfaced, and how might God be meeting you in them?

Prayer:

God, You are near to the brokenhearted. Help me to stop minimizing my pain or hiding my sorrow. Remind me that grief is not weakness—it's a pathway to healing when held in Your hands. Meet me in the tears and comfort me with Your presence. Amen.

Day 9: The Silence of the Hospital Room

Scripture:

"My God, my God, why have You forsaken me? Why are You so far from saving me, so far from my cries of anguish? My God, I cry out by day, but You do not answer, by night, but I find no rest."
—Psalm 22:1–2 (NIV)

Devotional Thought:

The beeping machines. The sterile air. The waiting. There's a particular kind of silence in a hospital room—the kind that stretches long and heavy. It can feel like God is distant, like your prayers are getting lost in the ceiling tiles. But silence is not the same as absence. Even when He doesn't speak, God is present. He's holding space for your pain, bearing witness to every fear, every whispered prayer, every tear. Jesus Himself knew this kind of silence and He didn't run from it. Neither does He leave you alone in it.

Reflection Questions:

- How do I typically respond when God feels silent?
- What does it mean to believe God is present, even when I can't sense Him?

Journal Prompt:

Describe a moment when God felt distant. How did that silence affect your faith? Looking back, can you identify any signs of His presence during that time?

Prayer:

Lord, when Your voice seems far and the room is quiet, help me to trust that You are still near. Remind me that even Jesus experienced silence—and yet, You were never gone. Strengthen my faith in the waiting, and let me rest in the assurance that I am never alone. Amen.

Day 10: God in the Fog

Scripture:

"Do not be anxious about anything, but in every situation, by prayer and petition, with thanksgiving, present your requests to God. And the peace of God, which transcends all understanding, will guard your hearts and your minds in Christ Jesus."
—Philippians 4:6–7 (NIV)

Devotional Thought:

There are seasons when clarity disappears—when nothing feels certain and the future is a thick fog. You pray for answers, for breakthrough, for rescue. Sometimes, the fog lifts. But sometimes, it lingers. And yet, something shifts in the praying. Not the circumstance, but your soul. God may not clear the path immediately, but He promises peace in the disorientation. Prayer doesn't always change things but it always changes us. Even in the fog, He is near, steadying your heart with His quiet strength.

Reflection Questions:

- What am I hoping prayer will fix right now?
- How have I experienced God's peace in uncertain or unclear situations?

Journal Prompt:

Write about a time when you prayed and the situation didn't change but you did. What did that experience reveal about God's peace and presence?

Prayer:

God, when the way forward feels hidden and the answers are slow to come, draw me deeper into Your peace. Teach me to trust not just in outcomes, but in Your presence. Change my heart even when You don't change my situation. Amen.

Day 11: The Question No One Asks

Scripture:

"Why did I not perish at birth, and die as I came from the womb?"
—Job 3:11 (NIV)

Devotional Thought:

"Why?" It's the question that echoes through pain, loss, and moments we never saw coming. It's the question we whisper in the dark, even when we're afraid of the silence that might follow. Job asked it. Jesus asked it. And maybe you have too. There may never be a satisfying answer this side of heaven. But God doesn't shame the question. He meets us in it. Sometimes, His comfort comes not in clarity but in closeness. And in that sacred space, we find that even without answers, we are not abandoned.

Reflection Questions:

- What unspoken "why" have I carried in my heart?
- How do I respond when God doesn't explain the things I long to understand?

Journal Prompt:

Write out the "why" questions that feel unresolved in your life. Don't try to answer them, just name them. Then reflect: what would it look like to invite God into those questions instead of waiting for Him to remove them?

Prayer:

God, I bring You my questions—even the ones I'm afraid to speak. I may never get the answers I want, but I believe You can handle my pain and my wondering. Help me trust Your heart, even when I don't understand Your ways. Amen.

Day 12: Mourning in the Midst of Praise

Scripture:

"Rejoice with those who rejoice; mourn with those who mourn."
—Romans 12:15 (NIV)

Devotional Thought:

How do you celebrate a friend's miracle when your own heart is breaking? Grief and joy often live side by side in the same room. It's okay to mourn even while you clap. God's heart is big enough to hold both your sorrow and your praise. In fact, mourning opens the door to deeper empathy and richer joy. He calls us to enter fully into the lives of others—whether in their celebration or their suffering—knowing that community is where healing begins.

Reflection Questions:

- How have I balanced my own grief while supporting others in their joy?
- What does it mean to mourn and rejoice well together?

Journal Prompt:

Recall a time you had to celebrate someone else's blessing while feeling your own pain. How did you manage your emotions? What did you learn about God's grace in that experience?

Prayer:

Lord, help me to be present—to mourn and rejoice with those around me. When my heart feels heavy, teach me to still celebrate the good in others. Fill me with Your grace to carry both sorrow and joy, knowing You hold them both in Your hands. Amen.

Day 13: The Unseen Goodbye

Scripture:

"Jesus wept."
—John 11:35 (NIV)

Devotional Thought:

Some goodbyes happen without warning. No last words, no hand to hold, no closure. Just a phone call, a sterile hallway, or a silence that lingers. In those moments, grief can feel unbearable—unspoken, unfinished, unresolved. But even there, Jesus weeps with us. He knows the ache of loss. He stood outside a tomb and cried, not because He lacked hope, but because He loved deeply. Your pain is not too small for His compassion. And your tears—unseen by others—are always seen by Him.

Reflection Questions:

- What goodbyes in my life still feel unfinished?
- How does knowing that Jesus wept help me process my own grief?

Journal Prompt:

Write about a goodbye you never got to say. What would you have said if you had the chance? How does it feel to imagine Jesus weeping with you in that moment?

Prayer:

Jesus, thank You for weeping. Thank You for showing me that grief isn't something to hide, but something You enter into. Hold the pain of the goodbyes I never got to say. Remind me that nothing is hidden from Your love, not even my quietest sorrow. Amen.

Day 14: Surviving Sacred Grief

Scripture:

"You keep track of all my sorrows. You have collected all my tears in Your bottle. You have recorded each one in Your book."
—Psalm 56:8 (NLT)

Devotional Thought:

Grief is not just something to get through, it's something God holds sacred. Every tear you've cried, every moment when words failed and all that was left was the ache, He saw it. And He didn't just see it, He kept it. Not one tear is wasted. In God's economy, even grief has purpose. It may not feel redemptive now, but survival itself can be sacred. The fact that you're still standing—still breathing, still trusting even a little—is holy ground. God isn't asking you to pretend you're okay. He's simply staying with you while you learn to carry the loss.

Reflection Questions:

- What does it mean to view grief as sacred rather than shameful?
- How might God be honoring my pain, even when I don't understand it?

Journal Prompt:

Reflect on how your grief has changed you. In what ways has it deepened your compassion, shifted your perspective, or shaped your relationship with God?

Prayer:

God, thank You for holding every tear I've cried. Help me to believe that my grief matters to You—not as something to fix, but as something You treasure. Teach me to walk through sorrow with the quiet confidence that I am seen, known, and deeply loved. Amen.

THEME 3:

The Process – Healing, Hope, and Holding On

Day 15: The First Step Back

Scripture:

"...to bestow on them a crown of beauty instead of ashes, the oil of joy instead of mourning, and a garment of praise instead of a spirit of despair."
—Isaiah 61:3 (NIV)

Devotional Thought:

There's a turning point in grief that doesn't always feel like healing—it just feels like movement. The first genuine laugh. The first normal day. The first moment you remember the loss without being undone by it. Beauty for ashes is a promise, but it's not always immediate. Sometimes, it's slow—like dawn breaking inch by inch. And that's okay. God isn't in a hurry with your healing. He walks with you, even when the first step back into life feels fragile and unfamiliar. The return to joy is not a betrayal of your grief—it's a testimony to God's restoring love.

Reflection Questions:

- What does "beauty for ashes" look like in my current season?
- Am I allowing myself to take small steps toward joy without guilt?

Journal Prompt:

Write about a moment—recent or past—when you noticed a shift in your grief. How did it feel to step forward? What role did God play in that moment?

Prayer:

God, thank You for being patient with my healing. I may not be where I once was, but today, I take one step toward hope. Teach me that joy can coexist with sorrow, and that every small return to life is a gift from You. Amen.

Day 16: Courage in the Cubicle

Scripture:

"I have hidden Your word in my heart that I might not sin against You."
—Psalm 119:11 (NIV)

Devotional Thought:

It might not feel sacred—the hum of fluorescent lights, the clatter of keyboards, the endless emails. But even in the most ordinary spaces, God is present. Your workplace can become your prayer place when you carry His Word in your heart. You don't need a quiet chapel to meet with Him; sometimes all it takes is a whispered prayer between meetings or a breath of surrender before a tough conversation. Courage in the cubicle looks like integrity, compassion, and choosing faithfulness when no one's watching. Even there—especially there—God is at work.

Reflection Questions:

- How often do I invite God into my workday?
- What would it look like to approach my work as an act of worship?

Journal Prompt:

Reflect on your current work environment. How can you bring God into that space more intentionally? Are there specific challenges where you need His courage or guidance?

Prayer:

Lord, help me see my workplace as more than a job. Help me see it as a field where You've planted me with purpose. Give me courage to live out my faith, even in quiet, unseen ways. Make my cubicle a place where Your presence dwells and Your Word guides. Amen.

Day 17: The Ministry of Showing Up

Scripture:

"Let us not become weary in doing good, for at the proper time we will reap a harvest if we do not give up."
—Galatians 6:9 (NIV)

Devotional Thought:

There are days when just getting out of bed is an act of faith. When you're not sure your prayers are working, your energy is gone, and your heart feels numb. But still, you show up. To work. To your family. To your grief. That's ministry too. God isn't measuring your worth by how strong you appear but by your faithfulness, even in weakness. Sometimes surviving is the victory. You don't have to feel brave to *be* brave. Showing up—hurting, exhausted, or unsure—is a quiet act of defiance against despair. And God honors it.

Reflection Questions:

- When have I felt like I had nothing to give, yet kept showing up?
- What does "not growing weary in doing good" look like in my current season?

Journal Prompt:

Write about a time when simply showing up—emotionally, spiritually, or physically—was the hardest thing you had to do. What kept you going? How did God meet you there?

Prayer:

God, thank You for seeing me when I'm running on empty. On the days when survival feels like all I can manage, remind me that even that is holy. Help me not to grow weary, and give me the strength to keep showing up—one moment at a time. Amen.

Day 18: Tears in Public Places

Scripture:

"But He said to me, 'My grace is sufficient for you, for My power is made perfect in weakness.' Therefore I will boast all the more gladly about my weaknesses, so that Christ's power may rest on me."
—2 Corinthians 12:9 (NIV)

Devotional Thought:

Tears don't always wait for private moments. Sometimes they fall in boardrooms, church pews, or crowded hallways. Vulnerability in public can feel terrifying—like you're exposing too much, risking judgment or misunderstanding. But it's in those very moments of weakness that God's strength shines brightest. He meets us in our exposed places and turns our fragility into a stage for His power. Your tears are not a liability, they're a testimony to His grace.

Reflection Questions:

- How do I feel about showing vulnerability in public?
- Where have I experienced God's strength in my weakest moments?

Journal Prompt:

Recall a time when you cried or showed vulnerability openly. How did God use that moment to bring strength, healing, or connection?

Prayer:

Lord, help me to embrace my weakness without shame. Teach me that Your power is made perfect when I am at my lowest. Let my tears—whether in private or public—be reminders of Your grace and strength. Amen.

Day 19: Healing is Not Hiding

Scripture:

"And the God of all grace, who called you to his eternal glory in Christ, after you have suffered a little while, will himself restore you and make you strong, firm and steadfast."
—1 Peter 5:10 (NIV)

Devotional Thought:

Healing is not about hiding your wounds or rushing through the pain. It's a process—sometimes slow, sometimes messy—with a timeline only God fully understands. Grace isn't just a gift; it's a pace setter. It reminds us that recovery isn't linear and that every step forward, even small or shaky, is part of God's restoration. You don't have to pretend you're healed to keep moving. Healing welcomes honesty, vulnerability, and God's gentle timing.

Reflection Questions:

- Am I allowing myself the time and grace needed to heal?
- How do I react when healing feels slower than I want?

Journal Prompt:

Write about your healing journey. Where have you seen progress? Where do you feel stuck? How might God be inviting you to pace yourself with grace?

Prayer:

God of grace, thank You for walking with me through every step of healing. Help me to trust Your timing and to be gentle with myself as I recover. Restore my strength and steady my heart as I lean on Your unfailing love. Amen.

Day 20: God of the Second Goodbye

Scripture:

"Because of the Lord's great love we are not consumed, for His compassions never fail. They are new every morning; great is Your faithfulness."
—Lamentations 3:22–23 (NIV)

Devotional Thought:

The first goodbye breaks your heart in ways you never imagined. But sometimes, life asks us to say goodbye again—to a hope, a dream, or even a person—over and over. Each goodbye feels like starting over, like losing something all over again. Yet God's faithfulness doesn't waver. His compassion is new every morning, and His love carries you through each "second goodbye." You survived the first. With Him, you will survive again and find new strength with every farewell.

Reflection Questions:

- How have I experienced repeated goodbyes or losses?
- What has helped me find strength to face "second goodbyes"?

Journal Prompt:

Write about a "second goodbye" you had to endure. How did God's faithfulness show up in that season? What new hope or strength did you discover?

____

____

____

____

____

____

____

____

____

____

____

____

Prayer:

Lord, thank You that Your compassion never fails, even when my heart is broken again and again. Help me to trust Your faithfulness in every goodbye, and to find courage to keep moving forward, knowing You carry me through. Amen.

Day 21: Cautious Hope

Scripture:

"May the God of hope fill you with all joy and peace as you trust in Him, so that you may overflow with hope by the power of the Holy Spirit."
—Romans 15:13 (NIV)

Devotional Thought:

Sometimes hope doesn't roar. It doesn't shout from mountaintops or promise instant breakthroughs. Instead, it whispers—a quiet, fragile presence that refuses to be extinguished. Cautious hope understands the wounds, the setbacks, and the scars. It's hope that walks softly through the shadows, steady and real, even when it feels uncertain. This hope is a gift from God, who fills us with peace and joy not because life is perfect, but because His Spirit sustains us through every trial.

Reflection Questions:

- What does cautious hope look like in my life right now?
- How can I nurture hope even when it feels fragile or faint?

Journal Prompt:

Write about a time when your hope felt small or uncertain but still alive. How did God sustain you in that moment? What helped you keep holding on?

Prayer:

God of hope, fill me with Your peace and joy today. When my hope feels quiet or fragile, remind me that even a whisper of hope is enough because You are with me. Help me trust Your Spirit to sustain me through every uncertainty. Amen.

THEME 4:

The Purpose – Fruitfulness in the Unexpected

Day 22: Fruitful Barrenness

Scripture:

"It is the glory of God to conceal a matter; to search out a matter is the glory of kings."
—Proverbs 25:2 (NIV)

Devotional Thought:

Emptiness can feel like a void—a dry, barren place where nothing grows. But what if it's actually fertile ground? What if this season of seeming barrenness is where God is planting seeds of unseen growth? In the quiet, the hidden, and the waiting, God is at work, shaping new strength, new insight, and new purpose. Like the glory of kings who search for hidden treasures, God invites you to explore your emptiness with faith, trusting that something beautiful is forming beneath the surface.

Reflection Questions:

- How have I experienced seasons of emptiness or barrenness in my life?
- What hidden growth might God be cultivating in these places?

Journal Prompt:

Reflect on a time when a season of emptiness eventually led to unexpected growth or blessing. How did that experience change your perspective on waiting and trust?

Prayer:

God, help me to trust that my emptiness is not wasted. Teach me to seek You in the quiet places and believe that You are working even when I can't see it. Give me patience and faith to wait for the fruit You are growing inside me. Amen.

Day 23: Birth Without Labor

Scripture:

"Shall I bring to the moment of birth and not give delivery?" says the Lord. "Shall I, who bring to birth, shut the womb?"
—Isaiah 66:9 (NIV)[1]

Devotional Thought:

Sometimes, waiting feels endless, like labor without progress. You expect pain, struggle, and then the breakthrough—the new life—but the timing doesn't follow the pattern you imagined. Yet God still delivers.

Not always through the process you expect, but through His perfect plan. He brings life in unexpected ways—sometimes quietly, sometimes miraculously. Trusting God means believing in His timing and methods, even when they defy all your expectations.

Reflection Questions:

- How have I struggled to trust God's timing and ways?
- In what unexpected ways has God delivered in my life?

1 Scripture study: https://biblehub.com/study/isaiah/66-9.htm

Journal Prompt:

Write about a time when God brought a breakthrough or answered a prayer differently than you expected. How did that experience shape your faith?

Prayer:

Lord, help me to trust Your timing and delivery, even when it doesn't look like I imagined. Teach me to rest in Your perfect plan and to celebrate the new life You bring—however and whenever it comes. Amen.

Day 24: Writing Through the Pain

Scripture:

"Then the Lord replied: 'Write down the revelation and make it plain on tablets so that a herald may run with it.'"
—Habakkuk 2:2 (NIV)

Devotional Thought:

Pain can feel overwhelming and chaotic, but putting words to it—writing, journaling, or even speaking your truth—can bring clarity and healing. Like a plow turning over a field, the pen can prepare your heart for new growth. When you write through your sorrow, you're not just recounting pain—you're uncovering hope, processing grief, and creating space for God's revelation. Your story matters, and it can become a beacon for others who walk similar paths.

Reflection Questions:

- How have I used writing or expression to process difficult emotions?
- What truths is God inviting me to uncover or declare through my story?

Journal Prompt:

Write about a painful experience and how expressing it (through writing, art, conversation, etc.) helped you find healing or understanding.

Prayer:

God, give me the courage to write my truth, even when it's hard. Help me to see that my story—my pain included—can become a testimony of Your grace and hope. Guide my words and use them to bring healing, both for me and for others. Amen.

Day 25: Your Story is Seed

Scripture:

"Very truly I tell you, unless a kernel of wheat falls to the ground and dies, it remains only a single seed. But if it dies, it produces many seeds."
—John 12:24 (NIV)

Devotional Thought:

Your story, full of pain, loss, and survival, is like a seed planted in fertile soil. It may feel lonely or buried beneath the weight of grief, but God is at work beneath the surface. When parts of us "die"—old dreams, past identities, or the weight of sorrow—new life (has the potential to) begins to sprout. Your suffering is not wasted; it is the seedbed for growth, healing, and hope that can multiply far beyond what you see today. Trust God's promise that new life comes through letting go, and surrendering to Him.

Reflection Questions:

- What parts of my story feel like they are "dying" or ending?
- How might God be using these endings to produce new growth in my life?

Journal Prompt:

Reflect on an area of your life where something had to "die" for new growth to begin. What new hope or purpose has emerged from that season?

Prayer:

Lord, thank You for turning death into life. Help me to trust that my story—my losses and pain—are seeds planted by Your hand. May new growth, healing, and hope spring forth in ways I cannot yet imagine. Amen.

Day 26: The Platform You Didn't Pray For

Scripture:

"Now to Him who is able to do immeasurably more than all we ask or imagine, according to His power that is at work within us."
—Ephesians 3:20 (NIV)

Devotional Thought:

Sometimes the places where we feel broken or vulnerable become unexpected stages for God's work. The wounds you never wanted, the hardships you didn't pray for, can become platforms where His power shines brightest. God is able to do more than you can imagine—using your pain and testimony to inspire, encourage, and transform others. What feels like a setback can be a setup for something greater. Trust that God's power is at work within you, even in the hardest seasons.

Reflection Questions:

- How have God's blessings or opportunities come through unexpected or painful circumstances?
- In what ways might God be using your story to impact others?

Journal Prompt:

Write about a time when a hardship or wound became a platform for growth, ministry, or influence in your life.

Prayer:

God, thank You for doing more than I can imagine. Help me to see that even my wounds can become places where Your power is displayed. Use my story and struggles for Your glory and the encouragement of others. Amen.

Day 27: The Tribe You Didn't Know You Needed

Scripture:

"For just as each of us has one body with many members, and these members do not all have the same function, so in Christ we, though many, form one body, and each member belongs to all the others."
—Romans 12:4–5 (NIV)

Devotional Thought:

Healing rarely happens in isolation. It often comes through the presence, encouragement, and shared strength of a community—your tribe. You might not have chosen this group, but God places people around you for support, to bear your burdens, and to remind you that you are not alone. Each person has a unique role in your healing journey, and together you form a body that thrives on connection and care. Don't be afraid to lean in and let others walk beside you.

Reflection Questions:

- Who has God placed in my life to support me in healing?
- How can I be more open to receiving help and community?

Journal Prompt:

Reflect on the people who have been part of your healing journey. How have they impacted your recovery? What might God be inviting you to do to deepen these connections?

Prayer:

Lord, thank You for the community You've placed around me. Help me to receive their love and support with open hands and heart. Teach me to also be a source of encouragement and healing for others as we walk this journey together. Amen.

Day 28: Redefining Success

Scripture:

"He has shown you, O mortal, what is good. And what does the Lord require of you? To act justly and to love mercy and to walk humbly with your God."
—Micah 6:8 (NIV)

Devotional Thought:

Success isn't always about achievement or recognition. Sometimes, success is simply obedience—doing the next right thing, day after day. It's a quiet, steady faithfulness that honors God through justice, mercy, and humility. When life feels overwhelming or your dreams seem out of reach, remember that success is found in faithful obedience repeated over time. This is the path God calls you to walk.

Reflection Questions:

- How do I currently define success?
- What would it look like to focus on obedience rather than achievement?

Journal Prompt:

Write about a time when small, faithful actions led to significant change or growth in your life or faith.

Prayer:

Lord, help me to embrace obedience as success. Teach me to walk humbly with You and to love mercy and justice in every step I take. May my faithfulness bring glory to Your name. Amen.

Day 29: Glory in the Graveyard

Scripture:

"Jesus said to her, 'I am the resurrection and the life. The one who believes in Me will live, even though they die; and whoever lives by believing in Me will never die.'"
—John 11:25–26 (NIV)

Devotional Thought:

Resurrection isn't just a one-time event. It's a daily reality that breaks through the darkest places. Even in the graveyards of loss, grief, or broken dreams, God's glory shines brightest. He breathes life into what feels dead and promises new beginnings beyond what we can see. Trust that God's resurrection power is at work in your story, bringing hope and restoration in the midst of despair.

Reflection Questions:

- Where do I need resurrection power in my life right now?
- How can I invite God's life-giving presence into my darkest places?

Journal Prompt:

Reflect on a time when God brought new life or hope out of a season of loss or difficulty.

Prayer:

Jesus, You are the resurrection and the life. Bring Your life-giving power into my dark places. Help me to trust in Your promise of new beginnings and eternal hope. Amen.

Day 30: Still Good, Still God

Scripture:

"For I am convinced that neither death nor life, neither angels nor demons, neither the present nor the future, nor any powers, neither height nor depth, nor anything else in all creation, will be able to separate us from the love of God that is in Christ Jesus our Lord."
—Romans 8:38–39 (NIV)

Devotional Thought:

No matter what you face—loss, pain, doubt, or fear—God's love remains unwavering. Nothing can separate you from His grace and presence. Even when life feels chaotic and God seems distant, He is still good, still in control, and still faithful. Rest in this unchanging truth: you are held by a love that will never let go.

Reflection Questions:

- How do I experience God's unchanging love in difficult times?
- What doubts or fears can I bring to God to receive His peace?

Journal Prompt:

Write about a moment when you felt God's love holding you despite challenges or hardships.

Prayer:

God, thank You that nothing can separate me from Your love. Help me to rest in Your goodness and faithfulness, especially when life feels uncertain. Remind me that You are always with me. Amen.

THEME 5:

The Pursuit – Dream again

Day 31: Purpose in the Pause

Scripture:

"For I know the plans I have for you," declares the Lord, "plans to prosper you and not to harm you, plans to give you hope and a future."
—Jeremiah 29:11 (NIV)

Devotional Thought: *(Another look at Jeremiah 29:11)*

Sometimes we run so hard after one dream that we miss the whispers of another. In chasing career success, I ignored the quiet cries of my body and soul until an emergency made me pause. What felt like a detour was divine direction as I surrendered and trusted in God, the author and finisher of my faith in whom I've committed my life to. It was in this commitment, surrender and devotion that purpose was born as the light of His word and grace showed me the way. In that stillness, I didn't lose purpose—I found it. God often uses interruptions to realign our hearts. What feels like failure might be formation.

Reflection Questions:

- Where might God be asking you to pause?
- Is there a dream you've been afraid to pursue?

Journal Prompt:

Write about a moment when failure re-formed you. What was the outcome?

Prayer:

Lord, thank You for purpose in every pause. Teach me to listen when You speak through stillness. Amen.

Day 32: Faith in the Fog of Grief

Scripture:

"Be anxious for nothing, but in everything by prayer and supplication, with thanksgiving, let your requests be made known to God."
—Philippians 4:6 (NKJV)

Devotional Thought: *(Another look at Philippians 4:6)*

Infertility pushed us to a deeper dependence on God. When the test came back positive, we celebrated answered prayer. But the joy turned to grief too soon. I left the hospital with empty arms and a broken heart. Yet even in that fog, God met me and brought with Him joy and unwavering peace. Grief doesn't mean God has failed. He walks with us through what we never imagined we'd face.

Reflection Questions:

- Are you allowing God into your grief?
- What scriptures are anchoring your hope today?

Journal Prompt:

Recall a time in which you felt the tangible presence of God increasing your faith to get through a challenging situation. Describe the experience and how that drew you closer to God. If you haven't experienced that yet, take a moment to invite Him into your situation or circumstance or life and ask Him to enhance your faith as you pray the prayer below.

Prayer:

God, thank You for being present in the silence of sorrow. Hold my heart and heal my hope. Amen

Day 33: When Hope and Heartache Collide

Scripture:

"The Lord is close to the brokenhearted and saves those who are crushed in spirit."
—Psalm 34:17–18 (NIV)

Devotional Thought:

Loss visited us again, and I questioned how joy and pain could dwell side by side. Yet even in repeated heartbreak, God's presence remained constant. He gave me grace to keep going, even to comfort others as I mourned. You can carry pain and still be a vessel of peace. God's comfort doesn't cancel grief—it carries you through it.

Reflection Questions:

- Are you giving yourself permission to grieve and still live?
- What does it look like to hope again?

Journal Prompt:

Write about a time God's comfort carried you during a season of grief. How did it feel trusting fully in Him?

Prayer:

Father, thank You for being near when life hurts. Show me how to breathe through heartbreak and still believe. Amen

Day 34: Fruitful Barrenness – When Pain Births Purpose

Scripture:

"It is the glory of God to conceal a matter; to search out a matter is the glory of kings."
—Proverbs 25:2 (NIV)

Devotional Thought: *(Another look at Proverbs 25:2)*

What seemed like an empty season became the soil for something divine. God gave me words in place of children. I wrote my way through grief and discovered a new purpose—one that would reach farther than I imagined. Barrenness is not always the end. Sometimes, it's the birthplace of a calling.

Reflection Questions:

- What fruit might be growing from your dry season?
- Can you let God redefine your idea of success? If not, what is standing in your way? Pray about it and let Him in.

Journal Prompt:

Write about a time you felt reborn after a season of drought.

Prayer:

Lord, make me fruitful even here. Let loss turn into legacy. Let barrenness birth beauty in my life. Amen.

Day 35: Redeemed and Rewritten

Scripture:

"And we know that in all things God works for the good of those who love Him, who have been called according to His purpose."
—Romans 8:28 (NIV)

Devotional Thought: *(Another look at Romans 8:28)*

Four years later, I don't just carry grief—I carry glory. National platforms shared the story God wrote through my pain. Not because I'm strong, but because God is faithful. He's not just the Author of redemptive endings, He's the redeemer of broken chapters. Your story may not go as planned, but in God's hands, it can become more powerful than you dreamed. Surrender it to Him.

Reflection Questions:

- What parts of your story still need God's healing?
- How will you walk forward—with both scars and purpose?

Journal Prompt:

Write about a time you surrendered your will to God during a challenging season.

Prayer:

God, thank You for rewriting my story. Thank You for using every loss as part of my legacy. May my life testify to Your faithfulness forever and point people to your Son Jesus (Yeshua), the Christ, the holy and anointed One. Amen.

Now it's Your Turn To Fill In the Blanks

Day 36: Hope Rushes In

Scripture:

"May the God of hope fill you with all joy and peace as you trust in Him, so that you may overflow with hope by the power of the Holy Spirit."
—Romans 15:13

Devotional Thought:

____

____

____

____

____

Reflection Questions:

____

____

____

____

____

Journal Prompt:

Prayer:

Day 37: Hopeful Delight

Scripture:

"Delight yourself in the Lord, and He will give you the desires of your heart."
—Psalm 37:4

Devotional Thought:

Reflection Questions:

Journal Prompt:

Prayer:

Day 38: Confident Hope

Scripture:

"Being confident of this, that He who began a good work in you will carry it on to completion until the day of Christ Jesus."
—Philippians 1:6

Devotional Thought:

Reflection Questions:

Journal Prompt:

Prayer:

Day 39: Rejoice

Scripture:

"Rejoice in hope, be patient in tribulation, be constant in prayer."
—Romans 12:12

Devotional Thought:

Reflection Questions:

Journal Prompt:

Prayer:

Day 40: Many Plans

Scripture:

"Many are the plans in the mind of a man, but it is the purpose of the Lord that will stand."
—Proverbs 19:21

Devotional Thought:

Reflection Questions:

Journal Prompt:

Prayer:

Dear Reader,

When you walk through fire, know that you are not alone. Every tear is seen. Every loss is counted. And every barren season still carries divine potential.

You are not forgotten. You are not forsaken. You are being formed.

God's not done writing your story. ***Keep the pen in His hands!***

An Invitation to the Resting Place

If you're longing for a place to pause, reflect, and breathe, the Resting Place is an extension of this journey. It's a sacred space for gentle encouragement, quiet reflection, and learning to listen for His voice as you heal and grow.

If this speaks to your heart, you're warmly invited to join. Click the link below or scan the QR code to enter the Resting Place:

www.intherestingplace.com

About the Author

Joy Butts is a Personal and Professional Development Leader, Strategist, Consultant, and sought-after Speaker known for her exceptional people skills and solutions-driven approach. With over two decades of experience working with Fortune 500 companies, she has impacted thousands of professionals through coaching, collaboration, and innovative leadership development.

A dynamic thought leader, Joy has served on the board and advisory teams of nationally recognized organizations and has been featured on platforms including Refinery29 Global, NBC, Good Morning America, Yahoo Finance, and PIX11. She is passionate about unlocking the creative genius in others and equipping individuals to grow in both purpose and performance.

At the heart of Joy's work is her faith. As a Christ-centered woman, wife of over twenty years, and seasoned business professional, she brings a deeply personal and spiritual perspective to leadership, strategy, finance, and personal growth. Whether teaching, mentoring, or speaking, Joy walks alongside others with compassion, sharing lessons on triumphing through setbacks, building values-driven businesses, and honoring the unique design of each individual.

Through storytelling, coaching, and consulting, Joy is dedicated to helping others grow in strength, purpose, and JOY as they pursue their dreams.

Connect with Joy Butts:

www.joybutts.com

https://www.linkedin.com/in/thejoyouscoach/

@thejoyouscoach

www.ingramcontent.com/pod-product-compliance
Ingram Content Group UK Ltd.
Pitfield, Milton Keynes, MK11 3LW, UK
UKHW041828200726
13854UKWH00002BA/875

9 798994 816806